Ayire,

NHANTINII RAM

ISBN
Paperback 979-8-89632-758-5
Hardcase 979-8-89744-631-5

To the one who I had in mind while writing these
words, to the recipient of these words.
They are yours more than they are mine.

Contents

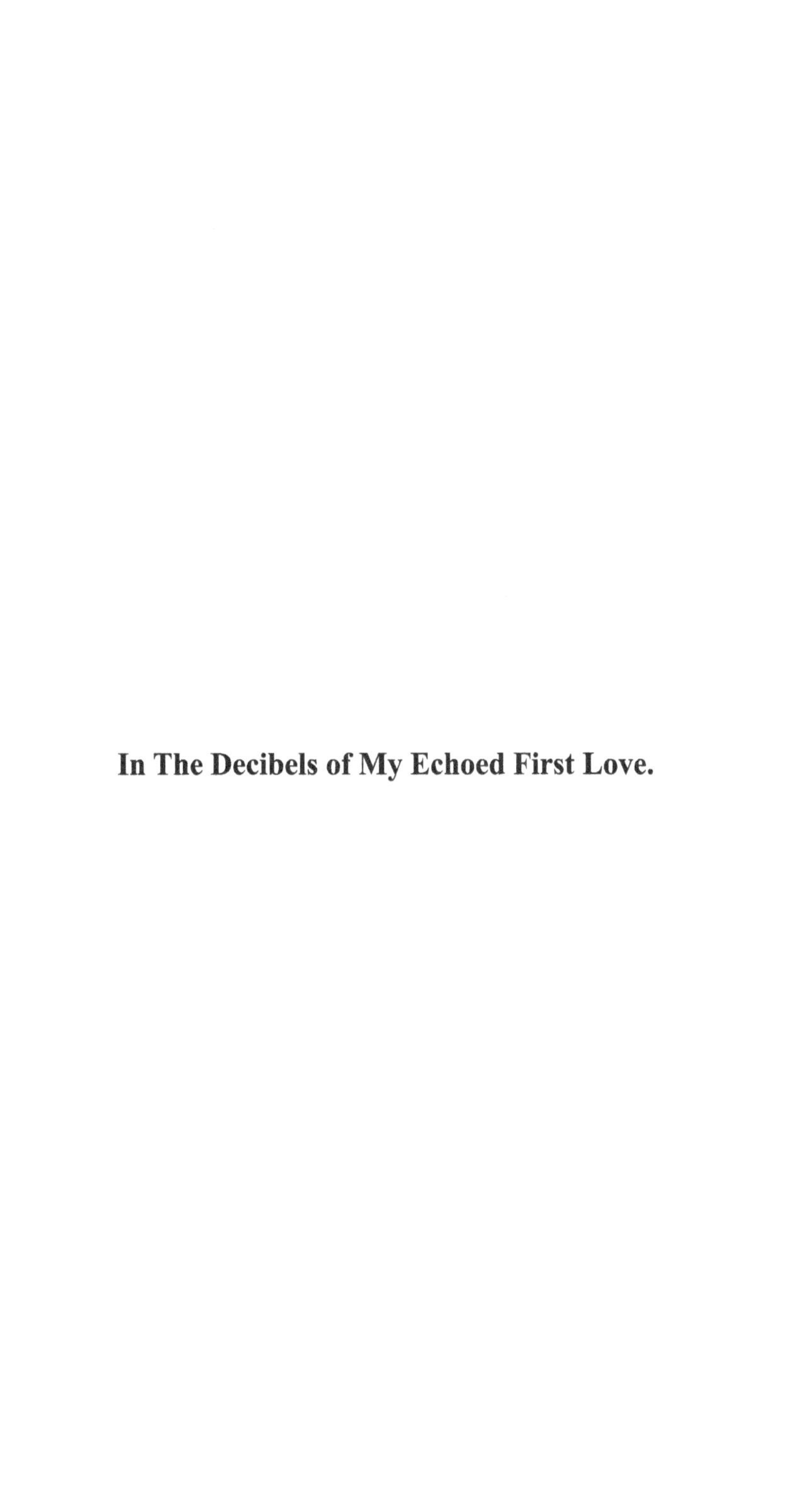

In The Decibels of My Echoed First Love.

01. Fallen

Why do they always say that they 'fell' in love? It sounds accidental, like something not meant to be. I didn't know I'd come to love you. But it was my choice to nurture it. I never fell for you, for I was already down when I met you. If anything, you held me upright, and I stood up for me and loved you for it. I walk, I run, with no fear of falling. And I will, inevitably, fall. What's changed is that I'm not afraid anymore. What's changed is what you've changed.

02. Aurora

A never-ending night, my world devoid of light. Suffering souls wander aimlessly, not being able to see what lies ahead, A torturous fight.

Unbeknownst to me, light explodes like fireworks everywhere around. My once-dark world is glowing, and flowers bloom in what was once a battleground.

I look around, unsure, seeing the you who is so pure.

You've shown me Aurora.

03. Butterflies in My Palms

Happiness can be so easy with you.

I can smile just like that and feel so damn beautiful doing so.

I can let it reach my eyes.

I can jump and dance and feel so free.

No guilt, no feeling unworthy, no thinking that I don't deserve it.

It leaves me wrecked in its wake because how can it be so easy to feel so light?

I have no other explanation other than the fact that it's because of you.

04. Whispers Between Me and The Night Wind

"Would I ever see you?"

I never spoke those words out loud as if they were a curse. But they lingered, a shadow waiting outside my door.

"Would you ever know that I love you?"

I never let these lines breach past my lips. But they stained, a whine quelled within my mouth.

"I can't love anyone but you?"

I never let this question step out from the comfort of silence. But it tainted, a weight that anchored my feet to one place.

"I want so much from you."

I never told you that. But it haunted, a ghost that followed even when the sun was high in the sky.

05. A Burning Flower

A flower that blooms in a desert. A splash of colour amidst the dull grey that traps the world.

Dealt by the hands of the unforgivable. For they were cruel to you, to those like you. Although, no matter how many times they pluck the petals off, no matter how hard they rip you apart; You're sure to bloom once more. Ever so beautifully.

(Just how much do you bleed for it to be a poet's shade of red?)

Your pain-wrought triumph travels to every corner of the world and attaches as wings to the back of someone fallen.

(Just how hurt are you?)

06. Shadows

I'm scared of the dark but not that of your shadow.

I care not for light when the black of your shadow welcomes me to its depths that I long to read, to learn, to decipher.

What no one else sees, what I could see if I am willingly made blind for a moment.

I want to know what about you is refusing to be brought to light and why.

The sun on your face, I see. The dark on your back, I yearn to know.

All there is to you to be etched onto the bones that hold me still, the blood that brings me life until it is not them but you that holds me still, that brings me life.

My existence that I want destroyed if it has to be without you. I want to grow used to the dark you carry until I can see it as clear as day.

Day, Night, Light, Dark; let me see all that you are just as you are. And if you'd like, only if you'd want, let me show you all that I am just as I am.

07. The Way You Are Known by Me

When I think of you, I'm completely alone.

No one knows the way you are known by me. No one is aware of what you have made of me.

The light of the sun is visceral, but no one knows what is engraved in the depth of its every crevice. How can they? To get that close, you'll have to burn.

To know that much, you'll have to burn. I've been burning in the flames you ignited for so long; I'm nothing but a mere pile of ashes that can't speak.

No one can get close enough to know me by way of you or you by way of me. They'll burn.

I, the burnt, have only particles of dust that mean so much to me but nothing to anyone else to offer.

They don't know.

It's a belief of mine that ashes remember their flames. I do. I remember you.

08. Don't You Want to See?

I would rather die than live in love with someone that's not you. No matter how much I hate myself, I could never hate the part of me that loves you. Not a thing of you deserves hate. Because of that part, I'm beautiful. Because of you, I'm beautiful. I'm so beautiful. Don't you want to see? See what you have done.

09. Thoughts

Please come. Come see me, please.

He left on a Tuesday. Waiting for the years to go by.

It hurts like a heartstring pulled taut.

10. Blooming Thorns

You showed me that pain never had to hurt. You showed me that pain was sweet bliss. When the heavens above were drenched in black, no one heard, no one saw as you touched me where my lungs were. Their motions were meaningless until the warmth from your fingertips seeped into them, and I came alive. Every breath I took in, let go, had your name on it. Time shied away from the sheer depth of what you caused to crash against the blood in my veins, only to become one with it as it flowed through my entire being. And time, I swear I could feel it stop when, beneath flesh and bone, white blossoms wept as they clung to the roots wrapped around my rib cage. I was a blooming garden that was planted and nurtured by you. You were soil, water, and the sun itself. The thorns tore flesh and scratched bone. The pale flowers with soft petals hugged every crevice, determined to swallow me whole. I bled for you because of you. I glowed with it. To me, the anguish was bliss. To you, unawareness was bliss. When the last drop of black fell to the ground, a blindfold was torn off. They showed what they thought was mercy. There was nothing crueller. And when you placed your hands on me; that was brought alive by you, I realised that the faint echo was not one laced with the syllables of your name but emptiness resonating back. You touched me; I burned with life. You touched me; I burned alive.

11. Your Passing

Why did you make it so that I won't even get to lay eyes on your corpse? Should I thank the gods that at least I'll hear of it? Several hours, a couple of days, maybe even weeks later, a stranger kills me when I've not yet lived with two simple words. "He's gone." Is that all I get of you? I can't even see your tombstone, let alone touch it. To trace your name marked on stone, my fingertips were not blessed. My goodbyes, I hope the wind carries them to you. However, I am not capable of living in a world that has lived past you. The footsteps you leave behind, my feet will walk on them, and they will take me to you.

My whole life, I did not get to live because if I ever lived, it would be with you.

I breathe because of you. I'm here because of you. My life is only until you die because if you left, why would I stay?

12. You by Way of Me and Me by Way of You

You are mine.

In a way, only you can be, and only I can make you be.

You are loved in a way that only I am capable of and in that, you are mine.

A joy that only you can cause, which is received and embraced by me in a way no other can. In that, you are mine.

The fear I feel because I am me and you are you and because it's us that this fear exists. Another thread drenched in a colour unknown to the world that wraps around us both. In this, you are mine.

Anger made turbulent only because it's you, and others can have such glares directed at you, but never like I do. In that, you are mine.

I am not the only one experiencing a multitude of emotions engraved with your name. I am one of many in that regard.

But in regard to my response, my reactions, my reciprocation, me, me, me, I am the only one in this world that can offer you me and all that makes me because I am the only me.

And only you make me this way.

In that, you are mine.

I will live not the same with you and without you. I will live either way, but with you, I am made into an answer that is only possible when you are a part of the equation.

All the ways you are, all the ways that impact all the ways I am. In the way how this connection will never be the same without you and me, is how you are mine, and I am yours.

It doesn't matter that you aren't mine on paper; it doesn't matter you aren't acknowledged and never will be acknowledged as mine.

It won't ever change the fact that you are.

You are mine. As long as we both shall live, things, thoughts, and feelings that are unique to me by way of you and you by way of me shall live, and as long as they live, you are mine.

13. My Passing

I'll die somewhere beautiful, thinking of you. Beauty is a sure occupant in a place filled with the thought of you. I want you to be the last image I see in my head, your voice, the last sound I hear, you, you, you, be my last everything.

I'll die thinking of you, so maybe I'll die thinking I was with you.

14. Pain and You Are Synonymous

I don't like pain. But most people would think I do, considering how many times I choose it. Considering how many times I choose you. Considering how I turn away the un-fought-for glee waiting on my doorstep. Pain with you and happiness without you are both just pain dressed in rags and riches. I shall live like this. I shall live in love with you and, therefore, never have love in my life.

15. Love to Me, Love to You.

I don't know you. That kills me. I am scared that I won't be able to understand you. That you'll be far beyond my comprehension. That I won't be able to love you the way you deserve. That my love may not be love because I don't know what love is. That my love may not be love because I don't know what I'm falling in love with. Not really. That my love may be love to me but not to you because love has so many definitions. That we might meet but not love and how could that be? If this is not love, then tell me, is there such a thing greater? Because what you've made of me could never be less, could only be more. How could I see you, have you within arm's reach and not-

16. Voice Note #1

Can I learn how to love you, from you? Can you teach me how to love you? Do you even know? I'm afraid I might be too in awe to ever understand.

17. To the Ones Who'll Ask

Tell me I don't know craving. That I don't know want. That I don't know yearning, longing.

And I'll tell you that you don't know how to breathe.

When you scoff and reply, "Of course, I know how to breathe. It's my nature; I'd die if I didn't know. It's not even knowing at this point; it's just something my body does without being told to keep itself alive. It's cognitive, unconscious."

When you say that, I'll look at you.

'Do you understand?' I'll ask.

Do you understand?

18. Voice Note #2

உன்னை விட்டு நான் வெகு தூரம் போகிறேன்.

(Leaving you, I'm going very far away.)

உன்னை விட்டு நான் வெகு தூரம் போகிறேன்.

19. Is Real, Real?

He had a smile that wrapped around my tired limbs and held them steady.

Should I say "wore" instead?

The fact that I don't know whether his smile is something he has to remind himself to wear is what shakes me.

20. Voice Note #3

வருவியா?

(Where are you?)

21. Her (or)

Is that her?

The one by your side?

The one by your side, in white, is that her?

I hope she's kind.

All the kindness the world has to offer, its rightful place is wherever you are.

If already scathed, ragged palms have an ounce of softness to give, they'll be yours.

I hope you love her.

You can never be happy if you don't love her.

I hope she loves you.

It's only fair; who wouldn't love loving you?

I hope she's careful. (With you)

I'll die if she's not.

Is that your little one?

I want to give her so much. What I have, what I didn't, what I will have, I want to give her everything.

I want her to be mine.

Alive with my flesh and blood.

Your little one.

I will take extra caution so as to not love her even a tad
more than you.

Can I be selfish for one last time?

I ask for a sliver of your happiness to be written off
to me. Let it be the thread that holds my tearing skin
together; let it be the mother that holds me to her chest
to silence my wailing that just might

rear the world deaf. That sliver of contentment; she can
never love you like I do. Endlessly envious, I

admit that maybe she has more of herself to love you
with, though it soothes me to know that never like I do.
Never like I do.

Please don't say that she can.

Please.

22. Let Me See You

If you're so set on agonising me, then at least do it while you stand before me.

Don't shoot arrows into the dark; maybe you might not know where they land. But I do.

Me. That's where they land.

Turn the lights on, let me see the sun; I don't want to burn black in the dark anymore.

If you're so set on agonising me, then at least do it while you stand before me.

(I'll tell you a secret. It can never be agony if I can actually see you)

It's selfish, really.

Because now it's not your fault.

But I want it to be.

Let me see you and then hurt me. I'll leave quietly. I will hold you accountable, though that too, I'll do quietly. You are responsible, quietly.

You're nowhere to be seen.

You're not mine to be seen.

At least, let me have you by you playing an active, visible part in my pain.

This hurt, they all say, is born out of nothing but my own only two hands. This, the lynchpin of my life. How can it be, though?

Make it real. Dignify my pain. I have loved you, and that is my pride.

Make it so. So, no one will ever say otherwise.

Let me see you.

23. I Want to Live with You

In my one life, barely more than a decade, I have lived centuries' worth of moments wishing you were there.

Like when I read a book and there's this one line that strikes me, and I turn to you, but you're not there.

I like to read. I'm writing it down here, though I wish I could tell you instead.

Like when I drive through night-hugged streets and she, with the murky moon and fading starlight, is flaunting her beauty so shamelessly.

Like when it's cold in the car, but the chill in my bones has somehow tired.

Like when I look at the driver's seat, hoping to see you, your open palm outstretched between us at the next red light.

Like when I try to curl into you, greedy for your warmth to sink into mine, but my hand falls through the air.

Like when I walk, arms swinging side by side, and I stop so as not to bump into you, though maybe I shouldn't have bothered because you weren't there.

Like when I was elated with a stomach full of delicious food.

Where can I tell you about it?

I win, I lose, I want to call you.

How can I?

I can't lie in double beds or sit in non-single seaters anymore because when I feel the coldness of the pillow beside me or the abundance of space around me, I turn to directions you won't be in.

Even if it's not so cold or if that space is somewhat filled, I still can't help but look for you.

Like when I live and turn to you, but you're not there.

Maybe you never will be.

24. Reddened Dreams

Red on my forehead.

Red on your fingers.

Red on the gold around my neck.

Red on my palms, my arms.

Your name in red, for you to find.

Childlike embers, utterings in an age-old tongue.

Them as witnesses to me standing red-written.

Behind my closed eyelids, within the burning black, the red is visceral.

25. Voice Note #4

வரமாட்டாய்?

(You're not coming?)

வரமாட்டாய்?

26. The Only Pained One; You Aren't

You are inhumane.

You see him hide small behind his outstretched arms, you see his knees bend, you see him fall. You see him writhe and claw and push to make it to the door. You see his movements fade out like a ballad that comes to an end. Still, you see him still-

Then he flinches; your stunted life restarts.

Only for him to lie on his back, and the tiles call to him as their own. Eyes closed, white sheet or not, it makes no difference.

And what do you do?

You turn away.

How are you anything but inhumane?

When all you want to do is take his arms, place them on your shoulders, carry your weight, don't let him feel it, not now, but give him something to place his weight on. Let the sharpened rain be the only occupant in the room when you drag him out. When all you want to do is not pull him up but settle on the floor and pull him close.

What do you have arms for if not to cradle him? It must be cold, you're not. He needs warmth. He has ears; you have words. Use them for anything other than him and what worth do they have? You want to lean over him, don't you? If the rain follows, let it rain on your back instead. Gentle kisses on his shoulder. Be anything but gentle with him and be a sinner.

The crimson on pale, pale skin is not the kind you want to see. You'd rather see yourself bathed in it than see a speck on him. But there's so much red. Red, you hate. Take the brush out of his hands, softly still, it's him, and throw it where he can't reach.

You can't erase; maybe he'll keep walking on the sunburnt concrete road, barefoot, like crosses on a calendar. Though, bringing him his shoes is something you can do. Maybe he'll keep seeing black even with his eyes open. To remind him that he lived past and through and gathered moments that reassured the breath in his lungs is something you can do.

You don't make it disappear. You're not a saviour.

You're a companion.

You aid to lessen his pain and strengthen his joy. Not let his fears linger lonely and not let his regret take him away. Not meeting his anger and not letting it harm you both. To make excitement a competition, to be more excited than he is for himself so as to always win.

To accept that he is them all.

But what do you do instead?

You turn away.

If lies were a kingdom, are you the king?

If loyalty were skin. A serpent, wouldn't you be?

When a child asks and asks and asks, "Are you the mother?"

"No matter what"

Changed your mind, have you?

Why do you do nothing?

Why do you do nothing?

Why do I do nothing?

Can shadows do anything?

They can only cry silently.

The only pained one; I am not

To be with the pained one, I can't

27. My Other Death

"A dancer dies twice, once when they stop dancing...
and a second time when they actually die."

I feel as if I have three deaths awaiting me.

The moment when you look at me, the me that was
robbed of the ability to recognise the me before you.

The me who had the foundation upon which she built
herself, be shattered and amidst the rubble found a
blueprint for new structures that you left.

The me whose sharp edges have been eroded into soft
curves that spell out your name.

The me whose hand's true purpose is not just to hold
but to hold you.

The me whose eye's one yearning is not just to see but
to see you.

The me whose thoughts of you fail to be subdued by
the rising or the falling of the sun.

The me who dreams of just talking and talking and
talking to you.

The me who is understood by Meera.

Your eyes, the same stagnant smile,

fall on the me who loves you when I reach my turn in a
queue, and you ask me,

"Who are you?"

I will die at that moment too.

28. I'll Love You

I'll love you with your black clothes,

I'll love you with your brightly coloured hair,

I'll love you with your slight hunch and small tummy,

I'll love you with your short height,

I'll love you with your bedhead and drools,

I'll love you with your sweat changing the colour of your shirt,

I'll love you with your upset,

I'll love you with your silly,

I'll love you with your gums showing when you smile,

I'll love you with your days when you can't stand.

I'll love you with your days when you can't sit,

I'll love you with your need to be away,

I'll love you with your need to be near,

I'll love you with your questions and your answers,

I'll love you with your stubborn,

I'll love you with the trophies you thought you'd win but didn't,

I'll love you with the trophies you didn't think you'd win but did.

I'll love you with your loss,

I'll love you with your gain,

I'll love you with you being the only one who looks away,

I'll love you with you looking right into the centre where hands pile up on each other after the years have been lived,

I'll love you with your every one emotion and every other combination,

I'll love you with what you cut away,

I'll love you with what you sow in,

I'll love you with the patchwork of your being,

I'll love you with your intersecting set of complexities,

I'll love you with your shyness and with your confidence,

I'll love you with you being your own person.

I'll love you but won't be afraid to take a different path sometimes,

I'll love you with me being my own person, too.

I'll love you with respect untainted by me.

46

Fill my silences with whatever you want. I'll relish in it all the same, as long as it's you.

29. Who You Bring Along

I miss my mother when she's standing right in front of me.

When I was clawing onto the side of the cliff, blood falling into my eyes and staining my view red, my heart ached to call out to my mother, to tell her I wasn't safe.

I smothered the voice and let go instead.

Because she peered down at me from above.

I had a sibling. I didn't know that it would hurt so much.

My heart ached to call out to her, tell her I wasn't safe.

I did. She left me looking for more people to call instead.

My dad tells me he loves me every day. In me, there is nothing left that is akin to affection for him. But betrayal snarls its teeth, and I spew black back at him.

He called out to me, heart aching and told me he wasn't safe.

"You can soften the blow,"

I have a mark not but smiles a many.

And that paints a picture that is just that: a picture.

I pry myself away so I won't cry myself away.

But to have a mother, a father, a brother, a sister and not to lose myself little by little, become someone I don't know, I don't like, I can't tell you how much I want that.

When they are the people I call when I don't feel safe, not the people that make me think of calling in the first place.

After all this time, enclosed within the walls I fought to shield myself away with, when I can't help but tear, I still, still, call out her name. I still, still expect her to come for me.

My mother.

She is my Mother.

But even if she came barrelling through the door, I'd still wait for mother to come.

Sitting in the place I've lived in since birth, I'd ask to let me go home.

I am greedy

Because when I say I want you, I don't just mean you. I want you with your mother, I want you with your father, I want you with your brothers. I want you with your sisters. I want them to be mine too.

My family. I want my family. I want to know what it feels like.

30. If I Could,

I think I'll ask to let me live inside you.

If I could, I think I'll ask to never let me stop holding you.

If I could, I think I'll ask to never let me go.

If I could, I think I'll ask to let me fall apart in your arms.

If I could, I think I'll ask to trace my scars with your fingertips

as I brush my lips against yours.

If I could, I think I'll ask to keep me safe.

If I could, I think I'll ask to let me shield you from harm.

If I could, I think I'll ask to let me be yours.

If I could, I think I'll ask to let me take care of you.

If I could, I think I'll ask to let me love you.

If I could, I think I'll ask to let me be loved by you.

There are many things I would ask you,

If I could, *only if I could.*

31. The Beautiful Girl

I swore off love.

If love came to me,

Lace hugging her curves,

An orange tint to her lips,

Warm water-lined eyes,

I swore I'd turn her away.

For when love inhabits my life,

I come home to you.

But she didn't come as love, did she?

Not at first.

She came bearing yellow roses.

Such tempting blooms they are.

To the lonely and the miserable.

If she looked at me,

A faint echo of your song in her eyes that lingered a touch too long,

I didn't think much of it.

For I wanted you loud and clear.

But she didn't look as love, did she?

Not a second.

We kept getting caught around the corner.

They softened into circles, and we kept going.

We'd talk like how we'd write.

And smile secret little smiles.

That's when I learned,

That she and I are the same.

That we were words moulded to look like beings.

She was everything I knew I wanted and didn't.

So, when she came to me,

Her heart beating outside her chest,

Red roses twined in her hair,

I let her in.

What was curious at first,

Temptation at second,

And desire at third,

Had run its course.

The wrongness of it all was overwhelming.

Now I write about you and she writes about me.

The loved ones never within our hold.

That's when I learned:

I can never love someone other than you,

I lack the ability to.

She was wondrous.

You are my love.

I hope to speak of her gently,

With you one day.

I'll tell you about the beautiful girl.

I'll tell you about her.

Do I seek forgiveness or

To keep the memory of someone who loved me for sure,
close?

I do not know.

32. Withering, Withering

I won't recognise myself if I'm not a person affected by your mere presence. Somewhere, somehow, you're breathing, and the knowledge of your beating heart keeps mine from stopping. Although, I wish I could be close enough to hear it. It's man's instinct to keep their means of survival close. Especially if it's the last one. I'm no different. I once said that knowing alone was enough. But the one thing time does for sure is wear someone down. I'm worn down. Now, knowing alone won't be enough. Not when I want to feel, see, hear you to know you're real. To know there's something, someone worth not giving up the little fight left in me rather than to just know. Only know. I want to touch. Knowing alone will never be enough, but it's all I'll ever get. The grip I had on your reflection (all that was ever meant for me) was not one that was as tight as I needed it to be. I wasn't someone who could hold you at all. Maybe that's why you're slipping away. It's getting harder to convince myself of the existence of something I can neither see nor touch. But who am I if not someone who believes in only you? Maybe that's why the farther I get from you, the more disconnected I feel with myself. I'm not in me anymore; I don't know where I am. If not with you, then there's nowhere left for me to go. So where am I really? Come see what's left of my body and soul without you. Come see me soon or come see me dead.

33. Blind Beyond You

I will live beyond you.

I don't want that.

God, I don't want that!

Can I save this hurt from time's healing hands?

I feel this pain in the absence of love. At the love worn deep into the lines threading across your palms being kept away.

If even that goes numb, what more of you do I have left? If it doesn't sting anymore, what of you would I feel? If not for the pain you so unknowingly give me, what more of you do I have left?

I can't have that happen.

Please, God, don't be so cruel as to not make it hurt. I don't want your salvation. Let me be damned for however long I have left to live.

I want to hurt for you.

You can't fade away like all of each thing is nothing.

I don't want you to go.

Wounds scab over. By me, they'll bleed anew.

"Adamant against the law of nature." It won't be the first impossible thing I've done.

The first: begging the one who heals to let me hurt so as to stay feeling so as to stay in love with a man who won't, who just won't.

34. Do I Still Love You?

When I sat down to write the poem about how I don't
love you anymore, I couldn't

I couldn't.

35. Little Things

Love can never exist on its own as it is only an
amalgamation of a hundred thousand little things.

A little spiking chill in my lower stomach when I heard
you were in trouble,

Heart gnawing a little hole through the skin of my
chest when I heard you were hurt,

Little strands of hair falling out to push in the lingering
arch of my eyebrows,

Strands I couldn't care enough to tuck back a little
when I heard you weren't responding.

Realising I couldn't care any little about the law or that
anyone other than you could've gotten hurt,

How I'd lay my principles, my values as the ground
beneath my feet,

But throw an axe at its centre when it comes to you - a
little thing.

A little frozen with fear for you,

A little clawed with worry,

A little dishevelled with unease,

A little maddened with instinct,

A little cracked with fear for me,

I don't know whether I still love you, but I have a
hundred thousand little things telling me that I still
care.

36. கர்வம்

I had never known pride until I knew you. I had never known arrogance until I knew you. I had never known smug until I knew you. I had never known anticipation until I knew you. I had never known frustration until I knew you. I had never known anger until I knew you. I had never known fear until I knew you. I had never known desolation until I knew you. I had never known power until I knew you.

And yet, every time you stand on a platform raised to the world's scrutiny, I welcome them all like long-grown soul shrubs with their woody stems encasing ribs.

A poked and pierced heart, swelling with pride, is what you've made of me.

And I shall continue to be so as you continue to be you.

An almost vow as I will never not be proud of you.

37. A Future Beyond Suns

I sat in the centre of darkened streets that were merely stained yellow by sun-shimmering lampposts, their cobbled tiles impersonating glass, and their water mirrors glistening.

I sat in the middle of it all, staring shut-eyed at the path that trails farther than the distance my sighs float.

I sat, silent in the only way a child that no one listens to can be.

Until you came, the one sun spinning enraptured circles around you, "I couldn't bear to part with him who dares climb up to me," she, the sun, said.

With you sitting next to me, the light from the lampposts dim, their shame ablaze.

You tell me about your home, and I built one on our street with a hearth in the centre akin to the pictures you painted of yours.

With you sitting beside me, composing the notes to my lullabies across flames that soothed instead of seared, I thought we'd remain.

But you got up one day, with only the metal you shaped to fit the small hole on my door nestled in my palm. I stayed seated.

Sprawled beside me, across flames that surged instead of sulked, the sheets of music you left behind caught fire.

I spilt the ink you taught me to write with, in an attempt to drown the burning parchment, ash black and smatter blue; they were a sort of grey.

Space beside me, across flames that sought instead of soothed, I thought would never be filled.

But the wind breezed in through the space underneath my door, it called.

With metal roped through and against my chest, I stood
and slipped out.

Down the path, through the seams, a flickering light –
not from the lampposts and not of the sun – spoke from
the opened windows of another house.

And somehow, I knew.

There is more than the home we built beyond and behind
me, though clinking along to the pulse of my heart will
invariably be the keys to our house around my neck.

I will love you always, even if I now know that I have
more love to give.

But indistinguishable will be the essence of our home
from my love no matter where it chooses to reside.

For our home is where my love was born.

38. Subtle Swears

I'm sorry I healed from the open wound that was my love for you.

I swear I still ache. I swear. I swear I stay leashed to phantoms. I swear.

I'm sorry I took the balm he brought and let his fingers stroke against the welts around my neck.

I swear I will not look away as your silhouette and its faint swaying wanes slow. I swear. I swear I stay holding out my arms in a lasting search. I swear.

I'm sorry I never refused his request to stand next to me and that I turn to speak with him sometimes.

You know that I still hope. You know. I can't swear that it's for you. Though that too you know.

I swear I will remember you; I swear.

So, fade free into the bending binds of a line drawn above the horizon, loved one; you will remain within my liveliness as I voyage across it.

I swear I will choose to care; still, I swear.

The sea can take you anywhere. I know now where I will end up.

I swear I will not forsake a thought of you, I swear.

With your oars in hand, I will splay my shadow over your doorstep to return them one day.

I swear I began through you, I swear.

And you can cut loose the tie it has to my soul.

I swear I will my end through you, I swear.

The Dents of the Sculptures of Him;

My Now and Forever Muse.

39. Muse

Stuttered breaths and stumbling words.

A gaze, playing shallow when it's anything but.

Your voice clanging against the metal in my ears;
nerves alight with a chill when you're standing a sea's
distance away.

A palm splayed on my shoulder atop coated, tweed,
and twill-woven clothes; my skin seared with an iron
brand.

Your words and their taste sink into the cracked skin of
my white lips, streaking them scarlet.

A thread poking out of your burgundy sweater; bestow
upon me the right to tangle and tie my limbs with it
forever so I stay engulfed in lingering lavender.

You turn to me; a pause in the way you look, a wait in the way you speak, a reach in the tips of your fingers, your sentences unsaid so starkly, your clothes feign crumpled in the places I wish I could hold.

Tell me the numerous wants of our one desire in a breath and a word.

Ask me what I want to ask you.

Ask me what we've both been asking of each other in everything but a breath and word; in a breath and a word.

Let form be derived from our breaths and our words so that they don't remain as mere breaths and words.

I want you; I do. You want me, do you?

In a stumbled breath and a stuttered word; ask me, ask me, ask me.

40. Witless Afternoons

I hate that you know me as a stumbling, stammering, wide-eyed fool. Because as soon as you move away from sight, I'm the smartest in the room. A quip on the tip of my tongue, an answer to every question, and all the questions to that one answer. I don't miss a step—anyone can testify to that fact. Well, anyone except you. Because, when you're near me, I'm a stumbling, stammering, wide-eyed fool. It's preposterous, is what it is. I should appeal—no, demand—that the cosmic court issues a warning: you. And it irks me to no end that I could match your wit as long as you're not there to smile like you do, and suddenly, I couldn't tell you my own name if you asked.

41. A Tulip to The Little Prince

All my love is doomed to die within me.

Then tell me why I keep dropping soul pieces on the train, heart pieces in my classroom, touching thoughts in the corridor, wailing whispers in the elevator, and clasping glances in the parking lot.

I cannot possibly carry all that is already in me and then you.

If all my love is doomed to die within me, don't fill my glass just to see me spill over sealed rims.

Unless you intend to soak your hands sore.

Then you're welcome to do as you please.

I might just drown you.

I might just draw you in closer.

I might just drag you through harsh currents.

Further and further.

Hew out my form wedged into concrete as you break the dam, my dear.

I might just fold to fit between your arms.

42. Teach Me the Ways of You

Would you watch the rain through windows, stories
above the ground?

Would you run into the middle of a downpour, arms
outstretched, and head tilted towards the sky?

Like they do in the movies.

Would you rush through the door, shut it behind you,
and close the curtains when it drizzles?

What would you do?

Would you walk the streets when the one sun sets, and
a thousand smaller ones shine in a line over concrete,
stepping unhurriedly and breathing even?

Or would you hurry along, hands clutching the straps
of your bag?

Would you return home as soon as the sky tints
orange?

What would you do?

Do you talk when you're watching a movie?

Do you hate even the crunch of popcorn at the theatre?

Do you care for neither or for both?

What would you do?

Would you sing along to the music on your playlist, the highway clear and speed limits; a gentle suggestion?

Would you hum beneath your breath and remain acutely aware of the soft tapping of your foot to the beat?

Would you remain unbothered, eyes focused, hands at 9 and 3?

What would you do?

Would you dance when the world dances?

Would you stand still in its centre?

Or would you sit in the corner and write about the people dancing and the ones who don't?

Like me

What would you do?

What would you say?

How would you deal?

When anger grows taller than the fences around your
mind.

Would you let it jump over and get to your heart?

When pain glues you to the ground.

Would you move away while it's still wet or stay there
for it to dry?

When fear rings a bell.

Would you answer its call?

When joy stays enthralled.

I know this. You catch it between your palms like one
would with a firefly, and when its small glow peeks
through the gaps between your fingers, your eyes
soften in mirth, and your smile cracks in a laugh.

 UYIRE,

This I know I love you for.

The others, well, I know I will love you for.

You love to teach, don't you?

So, teach me the ways of you.

I understand that a lifetime can pass, and I may not
even skim its surface.

The fact remains that I would never tire of lifetimes
spent learning to.

The fact remains that whether tired or not, I would
spend lifetimes wanting to.

What would you do?

With me.

43. Voice Note #5

I will command a next life into existence, and I will find you in it before they do. Until then, I will do everything in and beyond my power to keep you safe as for this life they have.

44. Single Checked

I want to take care of you.

I ache with the need to soothe your aches.

Let me pull you into my arms, dear heart.

Let me cradle you, press a kiss between your brows.

Look a little too long into your eyes.

Come closer; let me taint the space between our
breaths with my words.

Linger a lilt in the cusp of your ears.

I'm listening to the music you like.

Sing them to me, love.

Even if they're not about me.

At least let me take care of you.

Please.

I think I'll die if I don't.

Why do you stand, repelled?

I want to string out my being across the distance, but I
can't.

Can I?

Come closer, what harm does it bring?

Speak a little softer.

Though you already do.

Just to me, will you?

Merely exist always within my sight.

I'll exist exploring you.

Sweetheart, stop making me smile.

I'm too wry to be written again in love's smearing ink.

Don't blink me blue and braid pink in my hair.

I'll colour every other colour the same.

Don't laugh like that.

Don't ruin me for everyone else.

*Do you know you're all I look to in a room where
you're not even there?*

And when you are, I can't look away.

Charmed my eyes to never leave you alone, have you?

Angel, do you know how you look when you laugh?

UYIRE,

Like the man I love.

I love you.

Be mine?

God, please, why can't you be mine?

.

45. Twenty-Six Questions

Silent reckoning in the sill of a heart left to burn itself
out; a croak of life.

I walked with festering ash, searing my hands to ask
you a question.

Or two.

Or twenty-six.

You stood stone-like, maybe because you were carved
out of it.

With your arms held at your side, deft fingers
enveloping a beaded flute.

With your weight shifted to one side, your right leg
crossed in front of your left.

With flower garlands adorned, gems and jewels galore.

With your swaying, sealed eyes and knowing smile.

I could almost hear the jingle of your anklets.

The temple, your temple, never kept me away once
before.

Its tapestried columns knew how to hold me up.

Its bell rang alongside my voice, uncaring whether trembling or tranquil.

Its fire warmed the centre of my palm and caught the scent of my marrow.

Its grey shining gold never let me leave without a shy-seeming red.

I can almost say you know my mind as well as the one who created it.

It would make perfect sense then, no?

For you to know the answers to questions I can't even begin to make sense of.

Why would I meet him just to leave him?

Why does he let me?

Why can't I ask him not to go?

Why is he right there?

Why can I see him and talk to him, but he still is so far away?

Why can't he speak to me more, even if it's just to tell me about her?

Why did he, without his own knowing, make me alarmingly corporeal, only to hold me at arm's length as if to wane out my edges that curve towards him?

I will neither grow faint nor fade; does he not know?

Why do I trace the image of his hand when I see it wrapped around the width of his cup, harrowed day after day?

The one who came before him, that man, that wonderful man whom I deemed the one divine personification of love, I never got to see, I never got to live with, and I know I never will.

But him, he whom I get to see, he whom I get to live alongside though not with, he who will soon leave, will he not?

Why can't he remain within my vicinity?

Why does he intend to take himself away from me?

Does he know I'm unequipped to survive such a fate?

Does he know I do not wish to survive such a tale?

Does he know I'm here on my knees, begging him to please not do this?

Why is it so futile?

Why is it that I can't keep him even though he's right there?

He'll leave, won't he?

Why is it that even if it's me who walks away, it's him who'll leave?

Why is the only thing I know now for sure is that I can't leave him?

Why am I written to only ever know of love in one such ardent, aching way?

How do I love without these pages?

Why can I hold my love so dear within these words but never my lovers?

The one with ink-doused skin and a milk-white soul, won't you come down to earth and relieve me of my sorrowed doubting woes?

I pray for you never to make me doubt again, will you, please?

46. My Lord, Dear Lord

My Lord, Dear Lord, I am studying the lyrics of the
songs he likes.

My Lord, Dear Lord, why do they only call out in
heartache so acute?

My Lord, Dear Lord, why does his voice build arcs
intent on sailing through my cage-covered atrium?

My Lord, Dear Lord, why do they wail against the skin
of my chest before they seep in?

My Lord, Dear Lord, what happened to him?

My Lord, Dear Lord, why wasn't I there?

If only I had been born years earlier.

My Lord, Dear Lord, he smiles, and I see this wretched
world's saving grace imbued in its silhouette.

My Lord, Dear Lord, I don't want his forehead, his
eyelids, the tip of his nose, or his pulsing wrist to ever
be without my only-for-him soft kiss.

My Lord, Dear Lord, why does the joy he so readily
imparts part with him like a pulled-too-tight thread
snapping as soon as he leaves a room or is left alone?

For Joy to be smitten with him is a law of the universe,
I believe.

My Lord, Dear Lord, he's hurting.

My Lord. Dear Lord, please let me stand between him
and the world stained with the sin of harming him or
even thinking of such an act.

I do not know how to take care of someone. But all the
ways I've been taken care of, allow me to scrape them
off my skin and sew his wounds closed with them.

My Lord, Dear Lord, why won't he let me love him?

I've only ever prayed to be relieved of curses; he'll be
the first blessing I'll ever pray to hold.

47. Name Me Right, Will You?

I'm beautiful?

I am yours.

I'm loud?

I am yours.

I smile prettily?

I am yours.

I use big words for small matters?

I am yours.

I speak, and everyone listens?

I am yours.

I write rather than say?

I am yours.

I have too obvious eyes?

I am yours.

I draw strokes that tell?

I am yours.

I walk with half grace and half gauche?

I am yours.

I soften every gaze that falls upon me?

I am yours.

I live though killed twice too many?

I am yours.

Keep naming me as every other thing except the one I wasn't born but lived to be.

Yours.

Maybe one day you'll look at me and see that I have been yours since the day you never asked.

48. Voice Note #6

I'll try to exist a little less achingly.

49. Alley

In a darkened alley,

I scream, though it catches in the pulse of my throat, a plea for you not to do this.

In a darkened alley,

I yell, though it catches in the ridge of my tongue, begging for you not to leave me.

In a darkened alley,

I walk away, though my legs catch in the small space by the door, the door of a room you're still in.

In a darkened alley,

I can't walk away. I can't. You're still here.

In a darkened alley,

I speak, though my voice catches in the one question; your answers never linger long enough to be caught.

In a darkened alley,

I speak, though my words catch in only one too many sorries, your following smile is worth me apologising for lifetimes to come.

In a darkened alley,

I will remain curious and apologetic if that is the only state in which I can converse with you.

In a darkened alley,

I saw you once today, though you intend to leave me with an ache I'll etch into even the shadow of my existence.

In a darkened alley,

I talk to you, though you can't hear me.

In a darkened alley,

I want to keep seeing you, though I'm not meant to.

What am I to do? No one told me I couldn't even begin to deserve such things.

It was only you that I knew I would never be worthy of, no matter if I was God's favoured prophet or a king's first son.

In a darkened alley,

You're with me; you're here with me,

In a darkened alley,

How in all the three worlds do you expect me to walk away?

In a darkened alley,

I seek, though already found, I can't keep you?

In a darkened alley,

I pray, though already denied, don't leave me,

In a darkened alley,

I appeal, though given a verdict, please, don't take you away from me.

In a darkened alley,

I show, though you fail to see that I won't make it out the other end, I'll only sow my roots deeper into the soil pressed soft with the soles of your feet.

Don't do this in a darkened alley,

In a darkened alley,

Don't leave me stranded; I'll only get caught in a hollowed and darkened alley.

50. Lover

You are a poet's words.

An artist's mind.

A singer's voice.

A dancer's legs.

A student's teacher.

A teacher's student.

An athlete's age.

A doctor's instinct.

A farmer's soil.

For all those who love, you are the loved.

If I am the one who loves, then you are the one who makes me so.

In The Roots That Are My Family and
The Wings That Are My Friends.

51. Friendly Fire

Take this ash-grey love of mine and bring with it something that burns alive. I am aware that flames don't arise from ashes. I am also aware that phoenixes do. In what was thought to be done, burnt, gone, out of the sheer force of one's will, something alive arises from the clutches of death. Bright and blinding. Fragile in the heat of its strength. The ability to burn everything the sun touches, everything that revels in the fact that it is not touched by the sun, all lie in that unnerving gaze of chocolate brown. It unnerved me, made me uncomfortable, and put me back where I belonged. In the plight of all that chaos, I found comfort. Because it was you. Because to everyone else, you were what set everything aflame, but to me, you were that, and you were also what was amidst all those flames, fuelling it to burn brighter. To me and me alone, you were human, not some god-like force of strength. A display of courage. The adversity of imperfection. To me, you were all that and also sensitive after a long day of fighting, scared when the hands start gambling, and loud where silence thrives. They saw through you, saw what they wanted themselves to see. I saw you; I saw what you wanted me to see. You are what you want, and with me, you are you. Everything else in the world comes to me, and the vastness in my heart lives just as it is. You come to me, start fires in the empty spaces, and die along with them. Just when I think that was all you were, you rise like a phoenix from within. I should know better than to ever put a limit on what you can do and what you would do when you want. Burning brighter than the sun itself, trust only exists in my life after you became a part of it. And it burns.

52. For A Friend

Grown in my absence was a flower entwined with your soul. The part which I ripped out from mine and handed back to you. Be it not for my absence, it would have never bloomed. Our separation, the emotions we fought each other and shielded each other with, anchored it firmly within you. It was only a matter of time until the soft petals crowded your heart and coloured the blank bits I left behind. We're now both pieces from different puzzles; no matter how hard I try, we won't fit perfectly together as we did before. This was inevitable, this was a wave I knew would engulf me and take me far away to the depths of the sea to be left stranded, alone. Hurling towards the shore every other second, like a hand to reach when you're clinging onto a rope. The harsh waves pulled me back before I even set foot on the ground, like letting go of the rope and falling, falling fast. Then, I lose sight of the rope, my only chance at survival. I've given up; I go where the waters take me. Sometimes, it's peaceful, floating above the blues, soaking up the sun and letting it light me up from within. Other times, it's a storm. The rough onslaught of rain, like needles pricking my skin. The bombarding crash of thunder shook me to my core. The lightning and the fear that comes along with it.

The huge waves which threaten to drown, to suffocate. To wipe out the air from my lungs. But I let them have their way with me. Because it's better to hurt than feel nothing for you, because of you.

53. Paper to Ash, Ash to Paper

Piles of paper towering in the centre; you bring a
match, I bring a pen.

The match, your hands gripping one end, another
scratching a quick line against my skin.

The pen, I dropped it, trying to pull you further back.

But you walked, walked to and through the tower,
orange and blue paper flames in your wake.

You never stopped walking, with only one checked out.

I stand there, as red sizzles into grey. I stand there, as
ink melts and pools around my feet.

Before I knew it, piles of ash towered in the centre.

And when I came home that night, you told me you
couldn't see me.

My ashen, blurred being.

I never told you, "I can't let them go."

And when I came home that night, you told me you
didn't like what you heard.

My cinder-smoked words.

Ash in my throat, I never told you, "I can't let them go."

And when I came home that night, you told me that you hated what I had become.

My scorched soul flared once more.

You only ever have matches, and I only ever have paper.

I never told you, "You never let me go."

Please, *please*, let me go.

So I may stop burning.

54. How You Love Me

You love me with your hands and heart.

You walk circles around me, picking pebbles off the path ahead of me.

You speak words that are yet to leave my mouth.

You feed me morsels nestled in your palm.

You clothe me with yourself.

You build a beautiful glass house in a blossoming garden and stand guard at the door.

Come rain or shine, nothing reaches me.

You would bleed for me, empty funds for me, crawl to God on all fours so that he would protect me.

All this, you love me, you say.

But I remember the day I came to you.

I wish I didn't.

But I remember the day I asked you.

I wish I didn't.

But I remember the day I told you.

I wish I didn't.

You tell me you love me, though I make it so difficult.

I wish you didn't.

Because with your love, I do not feel loved.

I feel indebted, I feel trapped, I feel loss, I feel guilt.

You tell me you would never leave me alone, that you would follow me wherever I go, that you would find me no matter what corner of the world.

Smiling, you'd think I feel comforted.

I throw a cloth over the tremble in my shoulders, hold God in my heart and pray.

Pray that someday, I will feel loved when someone loves me instead of fear.

55. Indebted

It's been months since I lived in a house with people I felt safe with.

It's been months since I was touched by someone I felt safe with.

It's been months since I spoke to someone I felt safe with.

I will never get to, will I?

Because home will always be with you.

Because touch will always be with you.

Because conversations will always be with you.

And I never truly felt safe having you around.

I will have to pay off our debt with my life, won't I?

56. Voice Note #7

I'm scared God would turn me away and ask me not to taint his halls.

57. Heavenly Haven

There's a girl on the ledge.

She sits on the edge, feet swaying in the fall.

She turns, looks over her shoulder.

Eyes that soothe peer into mine.

Her warmth-reddened hands only reach out.

But I am beckoned closer.

She speaks.

Discord fading into clarity.

"Where I live, there are people who cry.

Houses that shelter,

Farms that nourish,

Libraries that enrich,

Gates that open,

Roofs with windows,

Meadows and marble."

I am a step closer to her than I was before.

"Where I live, there are people who smile."

Mothers who are kind,

Fathers who are just,

Sisters who are free,

Brothers who are trusting,

People bonded with heartstrings,

Friends and family."

Another step. Though now she stands.

"Where I live, there are people who shout, people who hide, people who scowl."

Walls that are bloodless,

Children who are playing,

Friends who are teasing,

Yellow streets with lone pedestrians,

Time and space for all."

She steps off the cliff, a floating figure facing me.

Would you be mad if I followed her?

"Do not cling to fear so tightly. It'll take you away from me."

I do not want to be away from you. Will you take me away with you?

"I'll gather and guide your soul as you come up to where I live. Leave your vessel behind; it has greyed too far."

Will you be mad if I do as she says?

58. I am my Mother's

"You'd make a great mother," you tell me as we play with the neighbours' kids.

"You don't think so?" you ask, confused at my chuckled response.

"One more second, and I wouldn't be," I say to you.

In answer to your questioning gaze, I say,

"When my daughter calls crying, she'll greet her tears safely cocooned in my unquestioning arms."

When she asks curious, I'll answer enthusiastic, leaving the thoughts of ignoring her as merely just that, thoughts.

When she screams scared, I'll bring her home and stand in front of her fears until she takes a step to look beyond me, still holding onto my hand.

When I make a mistake, I tell her. When she makes a mistake, she tells me. We'll be less, we'll be more, but we'll be alright.

One call, she calls me one time, and I'll come running.

She tells me, "mama, I don't want this," and I take it away.

She looks at me, "mama, get me out of here," and I take her away.

She weeps, "mama, I want to go home," and I take her home.

She can cry to me, she can ask me, she can scream to me, she can tell me, she can look at me, she can show me, she can turn to me, she's safe with me, she can trust me.

I will be her mother.

She'll know that; I'll make sure she knows that."

You turn to me, confused yet again so evidently.

"But one more second, one more second, and I can't be near her."

But one more second and our home will never be big enough for her, me, and all of my envy.

But one more second, one more second, and I wouldn't be a mother.

But one more second, and I'll turn into the child who waited and is still waiting for her mother to come for her.

"I can never be a mother, let alone a good one," I tell you.

"I'll always be my Mother's child."

"I'll only be happy if you have children," you say.

"I can never have children," I tell you, "I'll be so jealous of them."

"What are you waiting for?" you ask.

"For you, I'd rather wait for nothing forever than ever stop waiting for you, Mother."

Because to stop waiting for you is to accept that you'll never be here, never come close, Mother,

And I can't, I can't do that, you will, you will, you will,"

59. தோழி

One day, I burst in through the temple doors, much too giddy to kneel, and rambled on, "Do you know what happened today?"

One day, I stormed in through the temple doors, too grumpy to kneel, and huffed with arms crossed, "Seriously, this is your great plan?"

But on both of those days, I knelt before him anyway because, well, I had to thank him for sending you my way.

60. Soul Safe

You and I, we don't climb mountains, but you tell me
exactly what you'd bring, I tell you what you missed,
and somehow tomorrow we'll take on Everest.

And I know we could. Together, we could.

You and I, we never step outside our cluttered room
with a creaking door and one window. However, we'd
still nudge every secret of the vast world out of its
tucked crevice.

If Pandora's box gave us the world as of today, then it
also gave me the hope that remains inside, you and me,
safe in the sanctum of our home.

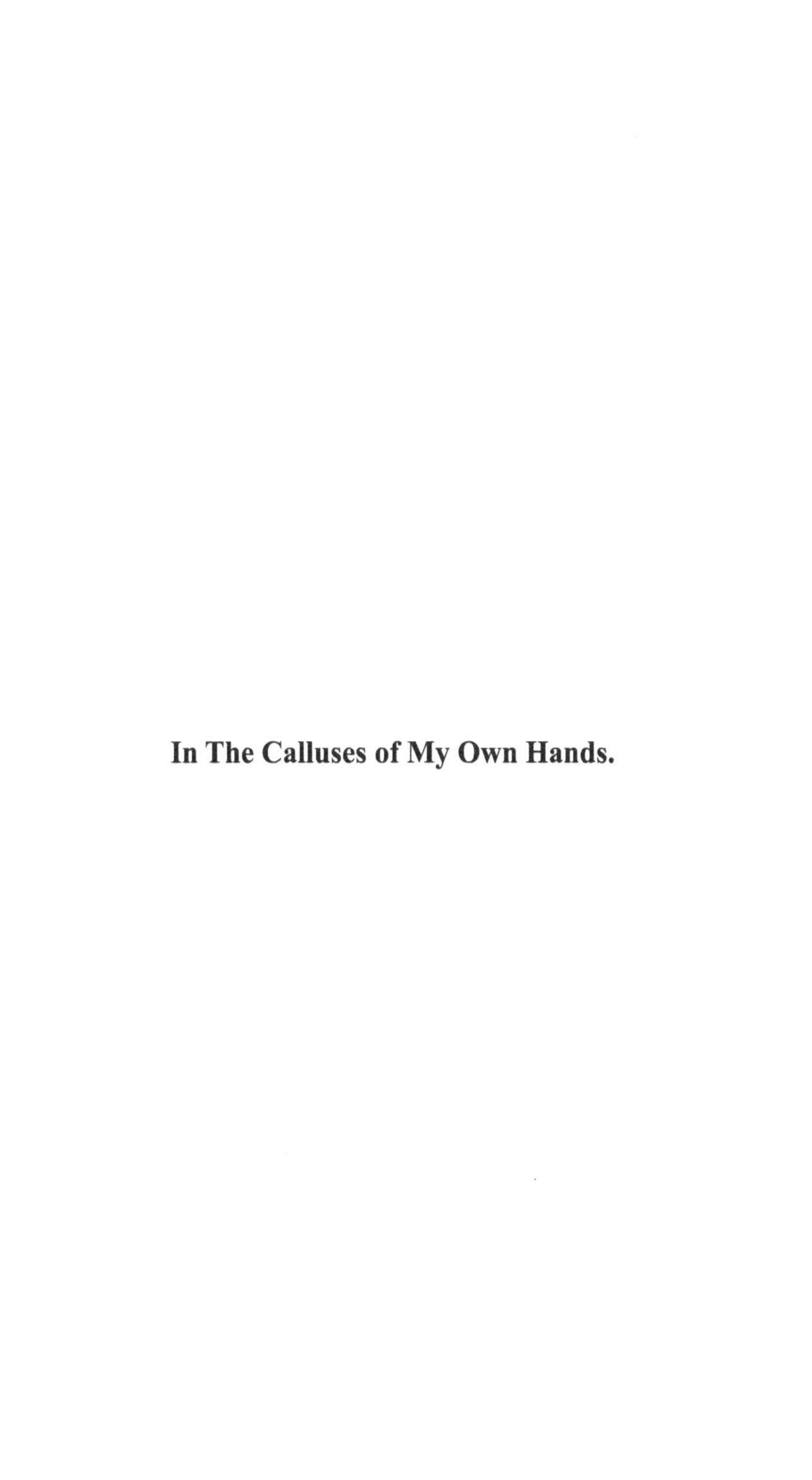

In The Calluses of My Own Hands.

61. Alive So Thoroughly

Most times, my body feels too small a vessel for all
that makes me, like if you caught the ocean in a net.

All that I see, the sights so pretty, the sights so pained.
All that I hear, the inebriated voices of one too many a
songbird, the luring lull of words. All that I touch, that
I taste. The poems and novels.

With nowhere to go but adamant not to be without
me, they settle in the left of my chest, the lump in my
throat, in the moisture of my eyes and on the tip of my
tongue.

When the confine that is my body grow too weak to
hold all that in, a few thread out in every shade of red
to wrap around my wrists. Unable to keep my hands
still, I weave them into a scarf that wraps around my
neck thrice.

The more I am alive, the tighter the scarf is pulled.
The hands that pull are those of my own greed. The
deliciousness of life has driven me delirious.

But barely held together at the seams, when my being
spills entirely through the age-brought cracks in my
body, I'm afraid I'll be a tangled web of threads no one
else can make sense of enough to unknot.

-

When I ask you to love me,

and I'm so much more than just me,

It's no wonder that you don't know how to.

62. The Mark of Life

I want to live. I want to live so thoroughly that my soul scrapes against the air and leaves marks behind. Marks that say I was here, I was *alive*.

I want to dance until the soles of my feet leave bloodied prints in their wake.

I want to write until the webbing between my fingers tears.

I want to scream until my throat shatters.

I want to live until the world turns its eyes to me in awe, and I shall point at one out of a thousand bruises gained from exhaustively indulging in being human to tell them how fulfilled I am.

That the moon herself called me beautiful when I walked this earth adorned with those bruises.

That when I marked life to tell her I was here, she gave
me in return – *her mark.*

I want to partake in everything the world has to
offer, to exist loudly and painfully, joyously scared,
vigorously and gently in love and grief: everything.

I want everything.

I want to live

I want to live

I want to live

So let me live.

63. Hunger

I give all of myself and somehow even more to the world and everything in it,

That if you were to give me the world and everything in it, in return,

It would barely scrape the surface of my need.

64. Everything That Once Lived, Rots.

There's a man on the pavement.

He's older than age.

A father to all things living and dead.

There's nothing he doesn't see.

There's nothing he doesn't hear.

And he sees.

He sees a house with four walls but no door.

He sees the lone window, sees through it.

There's a girl there.

He sees her.

She's in pristine white clothes.

Hair tied up and luscious.

Dancing and speaking and reading and writing.

She's smiling, and the books are where they should be.

The pots and pans are in their place.

The altar has a bright burning candle.

There are fresh flowers at the feet of her God.

Her God, not him.

The scent of sandalwood settles around her shoulders.

He leaves her be.

High up on his pedestal, he hears someone calling his name.

He climbs down and stands on that pavement again.

And he sees.

He sees a house with four walls but no door.

He sees the lone window, sees through it.

There's a girl there.

He sees her.

Her clothes were so brown, you wouldn't be able to tell they were white in the first place.

Unless you were there on those days.

He was.

Her hair's down and dried, scratching lines across her face.

She tries to dance but stumbles all over the place as if there's weight to her she can't control.

She speaks, but the walls or the floorboards or the crinkling paint on the ceiling, they don't respond.

The pen in her hand stays unmoving for hours until it eventually parts.

On the floor, rolling away from her.

She smiles but stops every few minutes to catch her breath.

The books have fallen off their shelves, and she moves to pick them up, only for another to fall again.

The pots and pans are on the loveseat, her bed, and by the fireplace.

The altar has a bright burning candle.

There are fresh flowers at the feet of her God.

Her God, not him.

There's something about the scent that settles around her shoulders.

And the call fades away, the voice no longer echoing.

He turns, moves, and time walks a couple more years.

High up on his pedestal, he hears a scream.

But it isn't, though.

It's the absence of a scream so loud, aching to breathe that it bleeds; he feels it.

He runs.

There, on the pavement, stands a man.

He sees three walls and the crumbling remains of a fourth one.

He sees through the gaps.

There's a girl there.

Her clothes were ripped and green with mould.

Hair crusted and in clumps.

She's on the floor, head hung between her shoulders, knees pulled up to her chest, arms with bursting blue veins around them.

He can't see her face.

There's not a book, pot, or pan in sight.

The altar-

The altar is bare; the candle has gone out.

The flowers have long withered.

He looks to the left of her chest, where, throughout the years, he'd sometimes see the same orange of the flame at the altar.

It's gone.

She's gone.

He knows the scent that clings to her shoulders.

How could he not, for a man who creates life and writes death, to not know the scent of decaying flesh is absurd.

She then looks up and sees him.

She smiles.

He then knows, knows that she knows he sees her.

He's not deaf. He has ears everywhere.

He hears the stories about the people who made their way into that house with four walls, one window, and no door.

About the girl who let her bitterness consume, and leak, and taint those people.

He has heard every telling of her tale.

But he remains, and he remains indifferent.

Because she needs him to be.

Because on the day her soul matches the state of her body,

On the day she stands in his court,

Waiting for his judgement to befall her,

Her one consolation is that at least he saw her.

He knows her tale as she lived it.

He knows her words as she spoke them.

He knows her mind as she knew it.

She believes that he does.

Because he is God, and she is his child.

After everything, and though she held someone else in his place,

He will be true.

Because God is true.

65. An Unlikely Group Makes Up My Being

To step outside the threshold of my home, my tired feet can't bear.

And so, they stay, me along with them, seated atop a hard-surfaced chair.

There isn't much that tells of a life lived in this one room.

Just a long Balsa table stretching painfully taut across the centre and five other chairs.

Fear sprawls across the seat closest to my one side.

She reaches out her hand, and I take it in kind, engulfing it in mine.

She laughs and tries to smooth out the worry lines wrinkling my forehead.

There's no need to worry, she says, as I'll always be here.

I could always feel her gaze on me, a soft chime of bells
in the back of my head.

But in the absence of it, it's as if the clock strikes twelve,
twelve times a day.

Trouble, why are you always looking away these days?

It's merely for a moment more, says Fear.

The ones inside stay inside.

The one outside, well, Anger circles the home once and
knocks on the door twice.

She's unrelenting, lingering in cycle.

Maybe there would have been space for you back among
the felt then,

but there's none today, says Numbness

And where is Numbness?

         UYIRE,

She sits at the head of the table, parallel to my stiffly seated form.

You'd think her quiet, but she sings monotonously, yet loud.

Her presence pushes into the finest cracks in the walls around us.

I'm here to make you whole, she says.

A loud whisper scratches across the record but leaves no marks behind.

I turn my head slightly and look at her seated figure, looming large.

Desperation sits restlessly, always fidgeting.

She's wrapped in a thick fur coat, leather gloves, and boots covering the skin of her hands and feet.

Hair inches long, tucked in a small but carmine beret, held back from summer's breeze.

She looks as if she's ready to bolt or scream but never says anything.

A hand claws at my stomach, and I follow the pale line of it to reach,

Hunger, who slouches in her chair.

She nibbles on the skin around her nails on her other hand.

I give her a feast; she turns away

They're not what I want, she says.

Her shoes beat noisily on the carpeted floors.

I am forever tuned to her every move, so I stand and walk.

She sits, familiar, on the only windowsill. I walk towards her.

She looks up at me when close; she should never have to.

I kneel before her, my head held low.

A hand on my cheek, a hand on the back of my neck, she tilts my face upwards.

And smiles graciously while I hug tight around her waist.

I shall belong to you in the most human of ways, for until Kalki swings his blade long after I've died,

I say.

So, tell me your name,

I ask.

You've known me from the moment you knew yourself,

she prophesies.

She's my sister, Hunger mumbles empty-mouthed.

I'm known as Longing to others, but to you: your nature, she presses against my lips.

Acknowledgements

Although the poems in this collection circle only me and all that is me endlessly, I would never have been able to bring it to completion or publish it if not for a countless number of treasured individuals. First of whom is my dear friend, my soulmate in the truest sense of the word, Uva. You were there with me when I started six years ago; you were there with me through all my worries and joys; you were there when I first thought of collecting my lone poems in the form of a book, and I know you will be there for the aftermath, no matter what it may be. Without you, I would have been scattered pieces on the surface of a million different things. You held me together long enough for me to do this, and I don't know how I'd ever thank you. To Mahi, Renu, and Harsh, who, in a short time, have become life companions, you three remain the only witnesses to the sheer chaos I endured to get this book out into the world. You reassured my fears and weathered my storms, and I can never thank you enough. To Madam Anu, my literature teacher, it was in your classes that I realised that poems didn't have to be a certain way or hidden deep in dusty drawers. The poems we read and discussed together, all those emotions and perspectives, I still think about them and will continue to do so for however long I live. You fostered the belief that poems are better shared in me, which led me here.

For that, I thank you. To Dainty, our time together was short in nature but it was due to you that when someone asks me, "What do you do best?" I tell them that I write and believe it to be true. You have helped me shape my work to be better, and for the time you spent putting up with my emotion-addled, rambling-like poetry, I thank you. To all the movies, plays, books, songs, and poems I indulged in, be it not for you, I would have never felt enough to have it splayed over pages upon pages of raw vulnerability. I don't know whether to thank or condemn you for that. And, of course, to all the inhabitants of the houses that are my poems, I thank you. After all, you allowed me the chance to relish in love, and all that falls under the term in countless different ways. So much so that I wrote a book about it. It would have never been possible without you. And lastly, to all those who held up a little bit of my crumbling resolve in passing, I may not be able to name all of you, but I will always remember that you are part of this as much as I am. I will stay immensely grateful to the lot of you.

www.ingramcontent.com/pod-product-compliance
Lightning Source LLC
Chambersburg PA
CBHW020550160726
47991CB00002B/666